INTERNATIONAL EXPRESS

INTERMEDIATE

Pocket Book

Liz Taylor

OXFORD UNIVERSITY PRESS 1997

CONTENTS

Other useful information

GRAMMAR

List of grammar terms

An **adverb**	adds information, for example, about when, where, or how something happens: *She wrote the report **yesterday**. He's waiting **outside**. Please drive **slowly**.*
An **adverb of frequency**	describes how often something happens: *I **always** play tennis in the summer. I'm **rarely** late for work.*
An **auxiliary verb**	(*be, do,* and *have*) is used with other verbs to make tenses and passive forms: *She **is** working in Geneva. Where **did** you go? The window **has been** broken.*
A **gerund**	is an *-ing* form of a verb used like a noun: ***Smoking** is not allowed in the office. He doesn't like **travelling**.*
The **infinitive**	is the base form of the verb (*come, go,* etc.). It is used with or without *to*: *It's good **to meet** you. I'd like **to introduce** you to a friend. I must **go** now.*
A **modal verb**	is a verb like *might, can,* and *should*. We use it to express possibility, ask permission, give advice, etc: *She **might** arrive late. **Can** I use your phone? You **should** see a doctor.*
A **phrasal verb**	has two parts – a verb (e.g. *look*) and an adverb or preposition (e.g. *after*). When used together, they often have a completely different meaning: *She's **looking after** the children. He **took** his coat **off**.*
A **pronoun**	takes the place of a noun: *The restaurant is very good but **it** is expensive. Do you know Sue? I saw **her** at the theatre last night.*
A **verb**	expresses an action or a state: *He **arrived** at 10 a.m. She **drives** to work. She **knows** the market well.*

1

Comparative and superlative adjectives

Form	Adjective	Comparative	Superlative
One syllable	low big	lower bigger	the lowest biggest
Two syllables ending in -y	busy early	busier earlier	the busiest earliest
Two or more syllables	modern enjoyable	more modern enjoyable	the most modern enjoyable
Irregular adjectives	good bad far much/many little	better worse further/farther more less	the best worst furthest/farthest most least

Use	Examples
We use *than* after a comparative adjective.	*The north is more industrialized than the south.*
(*not*) *as... as* shows something is (or isn't) the same or equal.	*Rome is as hot as Madrid.* *Paris isn't as big as London.*
a little/slightly show a small difference.	*Budapest is a little/slightly cheaper than Prague.*
a lot/much show a big difference.	*London is a lot/much less expensive than Tokyo.*

- One-syllable adjectives ending with one vowel and a consonant double the consonant: *hot, hotter, hottest*. This doesn't happen when the consonant is -*w* or -*y*: *few, fewer, fewest*; *grey, greyer, greyest*.

1st Conditional — *if* + Present Simple, *will* + infinitive (without *to*)

Positive	Negative
If I change my job, I'll move house. They'll celebrate if they win the contract.	I won't visit you if I'm too busy. If he doesn't phone, I won't go.

Question	Answer
Will you tell me if you change your mind?	Yes, I will./No, I won't.

Use	Example
Future possibilities and their results	*If car prices rise, sales will fall.*

- We use *can* in both the *if* clause and the main clause. *If I **can** finish the job today, we'll go away for a few days. **Can** you tell me if you change your mind?*
- *Unless* means *except if* or *only if*. *I won't contact you again **unless** there are problems. You can't use the club's facilities **unless** you're a member.*
- We use *in case* to refer to a less likely possibility. *I'll give you a map **in case** you get lost.*

2nd Conditional · *if* + Past Simple, *would/could/might* + infinitive (without *to*)

Positive	Negative
Crime might decrease if unemployment went down.	If we weren't so busy, we could go out more.

Question	Answer
Would you work if you didn't have to?	Yes, I would./No, I wouldn't.

Use	Example
Unlikely or unreal situations and their probable results	*If manufacturers made cars more secure, there would be less car crime.*

- With *I*, *he*, *she*, and *it*, we can use *was* instead of *were* in the *if* clause, especially in a more informal style. *I wouldn't go on strike if I was you.*
- *Could* is both the Past and Conditional of *can*. He *could* swim when he was six. (Past) *If everyone worked together we could reduce crime.* (Conditional)
- The past tense does not refer to past time in a conditional sentence. It refers to an unreal situation. *If he were the prime minister...* (but he isn't).
- We use *I wish* or *If only* + Past Simple to express a wish or a regret referring to present time. *I wish I were on holiday. If only I didn't have so much to do!*

3rd Conditional · *if* + Past Perfect, *would/could/may/might* + *have* + past participle

Positive	Negative
If the weather had been better, we would've enjoyed our holiday more. You could've come with us if we'd known you were free.	If he hadn't warned them, they wouldn't have known the risks. They might not have won the contract if they'd increased their prices.

Question	Answer
Would you have taken the job if the pay had been higher?	Yes, I would./No, I wouldn't.

Use	Example
Unreal past situations and actions and their probable results	*If the company had improved quality, sales wouldn't have gone down.*

- A past condition may have a result in the present. *If you had accepted the job, you might be in charge of the company now.*
- The Past Perfect in a conditional sentence refers to an imaginary situation. *If the company had improved quality...* (but it didn't).
- We use *I wish* or *If only* + Past Perfect to express a wish or regret referring to past time. *I wish you'd come to the party. You would've enjoyed it a lot. If only I'd known you were in hospital, I would've visited you.*

3

do and make

Use

There are no fixed rules about *do* and *make*. Generally we use *make* when there is an end product, e.g. **make a complaint, make a profit**; and *do* when the activity is an end in itself, e.g. **do a job, do some gardening,** but there is often no clear difference.

do: badly, (one's) best, business (with), cooking,* an exam, an exercise, a favour, gardening,* good, harm, homework, housework,* a job, photocopying,* sailing,* shopping,* sightseeing,* sport,* travelling,* washing-up,* well, work*
*We normally use *the* or *some* before these nouns.

make: an agreement, an apology, an appointment, an arrangement, an attempt, a complaint, a decision, an effort, an excuse, a fortune, friends (with), fun of, a good/bad impression (on), a journey, a loss, love, a mistake, money, a noise, an offer, a phone call, a photocopy, a profit, progress, a success of, a suggestion, a trip, war

for and since (See *for/since* timeline p. 31.)

We use *for* to refer to a period of time. *for five days/ages/a year/half an hour.*
We use *since* to refer to a point in time. *since yesterday/10 o'clock/1995.*

Frequency adverbs

   never   seldom   occasionally   often   usually
          hardly ever   rarely   sometimes   frequently   always

- Frequency adverbs go after the verb *to be* but before all other verbs. *They are **often** late. She **occasionally** phones me at weekends.*
- We can use *usually, frequently, often, sometimes,* and *occasionally* at the beginning or end of a sentence, for emphasis. **Sometimes** *he's away on business. I go to the theatre **occasionally**.*
- We can also use *rarely* and *seldom* at the end of a sentence, especially with *very*. *They eat out very **rarely**.*

Future: *going to*

Positive				Negative			
I	'm (am)	going to	leave. / start.	I	'm not (am not)	going to	leave. / start.
You/We/ They	're (are)			You/We/They	aren't (are not)		
He/She/It	's (is)			He/She/It	isn't (is not)		

Question	Answer
Is it going to start?	Yes, it is./No, it isn't.
Are they going to leave?	Yes, they are./No, they aren't.

Use	Examples
Future plans, intentions, and decisions	*I'm going to change my job.*
	He isn't going to attend the meeting.
Future actions/events resulting	*I'm sure the problem is going to get worse.*
from a present situation	*Be careful! You're going to fall over!*

● With *come* and *go* we normally use the Present Continuous. *I'm going to South Africa soon. When are you coming to see us?*

Future: Present Continuous (See p. 9 for form.)

Use	Examples
Fixed future arrangements	*I'm flying to Milan at 2 p.m. tomorrow.*
	They're not coming until next week.
	What time are you leaving?

● *Going to* can also be used for fixed future arrangements. *I'm going to fly to Milan at 2 p.m. tomorrow. What time are you going to leave?*

Future: *will*

Positive			Negative		
I/You/We/They He/She/It	'll (will)	arrive.	I/You/We/They He/She/It	won't (will not)	arrive.

Question	Answer
Will you start?	Yes, I will./No, I won't.

Use	Examples
Future facts and predictions	*Plastic money will replace coins and bank notes.*
	There won't be an election this year.
Decisions and offers made	*I'll get the information this afternoon.*
at the time of speaking	*Shall I ring for a taxi?*

● *Going to* is also often used to talk about future facts and predictions. *There isn't going to be an election this year.* In written contexts, *will* is more common.

Future probability

Use	Examples
Certain	*I'm sure prices will increase. Prices will definitely rise.*
Likely	*I expect sales will decrease. Sales will probably decrease.*
	It's likely sales will decrease.
Possible	*Unemployment may get worse.*
	It's possible unemployment will get worse.
Unlikely	*It's unlikely the company will expand.*
	I doubt if/that the company will expand.
Impossible	*I'm sure he won't resign. He definitely won't resign.*

Gerunds

Verbs + gerund *(He enjoys cooking. I can't risk making a mistake.)*
admit, appreciate, avoid, can't help, consider, delay, deny, dislike, enjoy, finish, imagine, mind, postpone, propose, recommend, risk, spend time, suggest

Verbs + gerund/infinitive *(I love travelling. I'd like to go to Norway.)*
hate, like, love, prefer, remember, stop

Verbs with prepositions + gerund *(She's used to flying. He insisted on paying.)*
apologize for, be accustomed to, be for/against, be good/bad at, be interested in, be used to, have difficulty in, insist on, look forward to, object to, succeed in

Expressions + gerund *(It's no use complaining.)*
it's no good, it's no use, it's (not) worth

Mass nouns

accommodation, advice, alcohol, baggage, bread, butter, coffee, equipment, experience, fish, fruit, furniture, information, knowledge, luggage, meat, milk, money, news, paper, research, rice, sugar, traffic, water, weather, wine, work

Modal verbs; *have to, need to*

Necessity/obligation	*You **must** be very patient. Men **have to** do military service.* *Do I **need to** get permission?*
Prohibition	*You **mustn't** break the law.*
No necessity/obligation	*You **needn't** eat everything. I **don't have to** make a speech.* *He **doesn't need to** get a visa.*
Advice	*You **shouldn't** use first names.* *We **ought to** inform the police.*
Possibility	*It **may** take a year to get results. The system **can** be frustrating.* *You **could** be very successful. She **might** be very lucky.*
Permission	*You **can** smoke here. **Could** I use your phone?* ***May** I smoke?*
Ability	***Can** you speak Portuguese? I **couldn't** see because of the fog.*
Requests	***Could** you hold on a minute? **Would** you book a hotel for me?*
Offers	***Shall** I get you a coffee? **Would** you like some more wine?*
Regret/criticism	*I **should have** warned them. He **shouldn't have** refused the offer.*

- The form of a modal verb is the same for all persons. *I/He/They **might** come.*
- To make the negative we add *not* or *-n't*. *I **cannot/can't** see him today.*
- We can't add *-n't* to *may*. *We **may not** be able to come.* (Not ~~mayn't~~)
- We put modals before *I/you/he*, etc. to make questions. ***May** I smoke?*
- With *I* and *we*, we use *shall* for offers, and when asking for and making suggestions. ***Shall** I call you a taxi?/Where **shall** we go for lunch?*
- To make questions and negatives with *have to* and *need to* we use the auxiliary verb *do*. ***Does** she **have to** work? We **don't need to** ask them.*
- *have to* and *need to* can be used in other tenses. *I **had to** work on Sunday.* (Past Simple) *I'**ve had to** do a lot of travelling recently.* (Present Perfect Simple) *We'**ll need to** discuss this again next week.* (Future)

6

Passives   to be + past participle

Positive	Negative
The problem has been solved. Elections will be held in six months.	Smoking isn't allowed on the underground. Prices weren't increased last year.

Question	Answer
Are safety checks carried out monthly? Was the problem discovered by engineers?	Yes, they are./No, they aren't. Yes, it was./No, it wasn't.

- We use the Passive when we are more interested in the person or thing affected by the action than in who or what did the action.
- If we want to say who or what did the action we use *by*. *Kansai Airport Terminal was designed* **by** *Renzo Piano.*

Past Continuous   (See Past Continuous timeline p. 30.)

Positive			Negative		
I/He/She/It	was	working.	I/He/She/It	wasn't (was not)	working.
You/We/They	were		You/We/They	weren't (were not)	

Question	Answer
Was he working? Were they working?	Yes, he was./No, he wasn't. Yes, they were./No, they weren't.

Use	Examples
An action in progress when another action happened	*Experts discovered that chemicals were destroying marine life.*
An action in progress at a specific time in the past	*This time last year I was working in Madrid.*
Previous plans	*We were going on holiday next month but we changed our minds.*

Past Perfect (See Past Perfect timeline p. 30.)

Positive			Negative		
I/You/We/They He/She/It	'd (had)	arrived. left.	I/You/We/They He/She/It	hadn't (had not)	arrived. left.

Question	Answer
Had they arrived?	Yes, they had./No, they hadn't.

Use	Examples
A past action which happened before another past action	*He had left when I arrived.* *She was nervous because she had never flown before.*

- We use the Past Perfect to indicate which past action happened first.
- We often do not use the Past Perfect if it is already clear which action happened first. *He left after I arrived. I arrived before he left.*

Past Simple (See irregular verbs p. 26 and Past Simple timeline p. 30.)

Positive		Negative		
I/You/We/They He/She/It	arrived. left.	I/You/We/They He/She/It	didn't (did not)	arrive. leave.

Question	Answer
Did he leave?	Yes, he did./No, he didn't.

Use	Examples
Finished actions and situations in the past Past trends	*I lived in Paris from 1980 to 1989.* *How long ago did you meet her?* *Air fares went up last month.*

- Regular verbs in the Past Simple end in -ed. A dictionary tells you when the consonant doubles (*travel, travelled*), and when the -y changes to -i (*study, studied*).
- When the infinitive ends in a /d/ or a /t/ sound (attend /ə'tend/, rent /rent/), we pronounce the -ed endings as /ɪd/ (attended /ə'tendɪd/, rented /'rentɪd/).

Present Continuous

Positive			Negative		
I	'm (am)		I	'm not (am not)	
You/We/They	're (are)	leaving.	You/We/They	aren't (are not)	leaving.
He/She/It	's (is)		He/She/It	isn't (is not)	

Question	Answer
Are you leaving? Is she leaving?	Yes, I am./No, I'm not. Yes, she is./No, she isn't.

Use	Examples
Actions happening now Temporary situations or actions Present trends Fixed future arrangements	*He's talking to a visitor.* *They're attending a training course.* *House prices are falling.* *I'm flying to New York tomorrow.*

Present Perfect Continuous (See Present Perfect Continuous timeline p. 31.)

Positive			Negative		
I/You/ We/They	've (have)	been working.	I/You/ We/They	haven't (have not)	been working.
He/She/It	's (has)		He/She/It	hasn't (has not)	

Answer	Question
Has he been working? Have they been running?	Yes, he has./No, he hasn't. Yes, they have./No, they haven't.

Use	Examples
Activities that began in the past and continue to the present Activities that began in the past and have just stopped	*Scientists have been trying to solve the* *problem for years.* *That smells good! What have you been* *cooking?*

- We often use the continuous form to focus on an activity rather than its result. *I've been fixing the car.* (My hands are dirty.) *I've fixed the car.* (Now I can drive to work.)
- The continuous form can also suggest that an activity will continue. *Venice has been sinking for years.* (It's still sinking.) *I've been working for my company for six years.* (I will continue to work there.)

Present Perfect Simple (See Present Perfect Simple timelines p. 31.)

Positive			Negative		
I/You/We/They	've (have)	worked.	I/You/We/They	haven't (have not)	worked.
He/She/It	's (has)	left.	He/She/It	hasn't (has not)	left.

Question	Answer
Have you worked?	Yes, I have./No, I haven't.
Has it worked?	Yes, it has./No, it hasn't.

Use	Examples
Situations that began in the past and continue to the present	He's been a diplomat for fifteen years. Venice has always had floods.
Situations and actions in a time up to the present	She's lived in several different countries. They've built factories all over the world.
Past actions with results in the present	He's broken his leg. The sea level has risen.
Past actions in a time up to the present where we give a quantity	How many cars have you sold this year? I've written three reports this week.

- In British English the Present Perfect Simple is normally used with *just, already, yet, recently,* and *ever. They haven't moved house **yet**. I've **just** returned from Denmark.* In American English the Past Simple may be used.

Present Simple

Positive			Negative		
I/You/We/They	work.		I/You/We/They	don't (do not)	work.
He/She/It	works.		He/She/It	doesn't (does not)	

Question	Answer
Do you work?	Yes, I do./No, I don't.
Does he work?	Yes, he does./No, he doesn't.

Use	Examples
Long-term situations	She lives in Stockholm.
Habits and routines	How often do you go abroad?
Feelings and opinions	I don't like spicy food.
Facts	It rains a lot in the spring.
Timetables and programmes	The train arrives at 18.20.

Relative clauses

Defining relative clauses

Use	Examples
Who/that/ whom*for people	*The candidate who/that got the job was Norwegian.*
	The applicant who/that/whom* we saw was well-qualified.
Which/that for things	*The car which/that broke down had cost a fortune.*
	The house which/that they own dates from the 16th century.
Where for places	*I'd like to live in a city where the air is not polluted.*
Whose for people	*I met a woman whose husband knows you.*

- *Whom**is mainly used in formal, written English.
- *Who*, *that*, and *which* can be omitted when they are the object of the verb in the relative clause.
- *Whose* can also be used for places and things. *France is a country whose food is well-known internationally.*

Non-defining relative clauses

Use	Examples
Who/whom*for people	*His daughter, who lives in Canada, is a famous actress.*
Which for things	*I stayed at the Moat Hotel, which was recommended by a friend.*
Where for places	*He's returning to Mexico, where he was born.*
Whose for people	*My boss, whose children are grown up, wants to retire abroad.*

- *Whom**is mainly used in formal, written English.
- *That* cannot be used in a non-defining relative clause.
- *Who* or *which* cannot be omitted.
- Commas are used to separate the relative clause from the rest of the sentence.
- *Whose* can also be used for places and things. *Seoul, whose population is 10 million, is the capital of South Korea.*

Reported speech

Direct statement		Reported statement
'Prices usually **go up** in spring,' she told me. (Present Simple)	➡	She told me (that) prices usually **went up** in spring. (Past Simple)
'We're **expanding** into Eastern Europe,' he said. (Present Continuous)	➡	He said the company **was expanding** into Eastern Europe. (Past Continuous)
'The plane **arrived** late,' she explained. (Past Simple)	➡	She explained that the plane **had arrived** late. (Past Perfect)
'We **haven't sold** the company,' they told the staff. (Present Perfect)	➡	They told the staff they **hadn't sold** the company. (Past Perfect)
'I'll **fax** the information,' he promised. (*will*)	➡	He promised he **would fax** the information. (*would*)
'We **can increase** salaries,' they announced. (*can*)	➡	They announced they **could increase** salaries. (*could*)

- When reporting verbs are in the past tense, the verbs of the original speech usually 'move back' one tense when reported. *'Nothing valuable **has been** stolen.'* *He told reporters nothing valuable **had been** stolen.*
- When the reporting verb is in the present tense there is no change in the verb tense when reported. *'There'll be a delay.'* *He says there'll be a delay.*
- In spoken language the tense may stay the same in reported speech, especially if the statement is still true. *'I live in Paris.'* *She told me she lives in Paris.*
- Sometimes the idea is reported rather than the actual words. *'I'm not going to say anything.'* *He refused to say anything.*
- *Tell* is followed by an object. *They told **them** to leave.*
- *Would, should, might,* and *could* stay the same in reported speech.
- *Must* may stay the same, or change to *had to.*
- *May* may stay the same, or change to *might.*
- Time references change if they are no longer true in reported speech.

Direct speech	Reported speech
today	that day
this morning	that morning
tomorrow	the next/following day
next week	the next/following week
yesterday	the day before/the previous day
last week	the week before/the previous week

Direct question		Reported question
'Where **are** you **staying**?'	➡	He asked me where I **was staying**.
'What **has happened**?'	➡	They wanted to know what **had happened**.
'Will you visit us tomorrow?'	➡	They asked me if I **would visit** them the next day.
'Can you solve the problem?'	➡	She asked if I **could solve** the problem.

- Reported questions do not have the word order of direct questions and the auxiliary (*do, does, did,* etc.) is no longer necessary. *'Where do you work?' He asked me where I worked.* (Not ~~He asked me where did I work.~~)
- When there is no *Wh-* question word in the direct question, *if* or *whether* is used in the reported question. *'Have you lived abroad?' She asked me **if/whether** I had lived abroad.*

Direct order/request		Reported order/request
'Stay in bed for a week.'	➡	The doctor told her to stay in bed for a week.
'Don't cause any trouble.'	➡	He told them not to cause any trouble.
'Could you sign the letter?'	➡	She asked him to sign the letter.

State verbs

Verbs of feeling and thinking
like, love, want, prefer, dislike,
hate, appreciate, think*, know,
believe, understand, forget,
remember, mean, realize, recognize

Verbs of sense
hear, see*, taste*, smell*, feel*
Other verbs
own, have*, be*, belong,
consist of, contain, exist, include

- State verbs are not normally used in the continuous form.
- We often use *can* with verbs of sense. *I can smell something burning.*
  Can you hear that noise?
- *We can use some verbs in the continuous form, often with a different meaning.
  I'm seeing (meeting) *her at 11 a.m. I see* (understand) *what you mean.*

Subject and object questions

Who and *what* can be the subject or the object of a question. There is no auxiliary verb or inversion in subject questions as there is in object questions. We use an auxiliary verb in the answer to a subject question.

Who *did Ricardo* **inherit** *the company from?* (object question)   (*From his father.*)
Who **inherited** *the company?* (subject question)   (*Ricardo* **did**.)

What *do employees* **vote** *on?* (object question)   (*On big decisions.*)
What **changed** *in 1980?* (subject question)   (*Semco* **did**.)

Time clauses

Use	Examples
We use the Present Simple to express the future in time clauses beginning with *when, as soon as, before, after,* and (*not*) *until*.	*I'll leave as soon as I finish.* *I won't make any changes until you agree.* *Will you phone me when you get to the hotel?*

- We can also use the Present Perfect Simple in future time clauses. *I'll leave* **as soon as** *I've finished. I won't make any changes* **until** *you've agreed.*

used to

Positive			Negative		
I/You/We/They He/She	used to	smoke.	I/You/We/They He/She	didn't use to	smoke.

Question	Answer
Did you use to smoke?	Yes, I did./No, I didn't.

Use	Examples
Repeated actions in the past Past states	*I used to jog two hours a day.* *He used to be a professional footballer.*

- We use *used to* to emphasize that the past action or state is no longer true. *I **used to** do a lot of sport.* (But I do very little now.)
- Note the difference between *I **used to** live in the city centre.* (I don't now.) and *I am **used to** living in the city centre.* (I am accustomed to it.)

SOCIAL AND FUNCTIONAL ENGLISH (S=strong, T=tentative. All other forms=neutral)

Advice and suggestions

Asking for advice and suggestions

What would you | advise us to do?
              | suggest?

What do you recommend?

I'd like to hear your ideas on this.

Do you have any suggestions?

Do you think we should... (*hire a consultant*)?

Giving advice and suggestions

I'd | recommend (that)... (*we consult an expert*).
    | suggest

I | recommend... (*getting expert advice*).
  | suggest

My advice would be to... (*ask a lawyer*).

If I were you I'd... (*advertise on TV*).

I think you should... (*increase prices*).

Have you thought of... (*selling abroad*)?

Why don't we... (*delay production*)?

How about... (*asking local people*)?

You could... (*employ more staff*). (T)

It might be a good idea to... (*do more research*). (T)

Accepting

Yes, I'm definitely in favour of doing that. (S)

Yes, I think we should do that.

Yes, that's an interesting idea.

Yes, that sounds like a good idea.

Yes, let's do that.

Rejecting

I'm sorry, but that's out of the question. (S)

I'm afraid I'm not very keen on that idea.

I'm not sure about that.

That's very interesting but... (*it's too complicated*).

No,... (*I don't think that will work*).

Explaining the reason for writing

I am writing to | enquire about... (*your latest product range*).
                 | inform you that... (*we are moving office*).
                 | confirm... (*the details of our recent discussion*).

Making reference

With reference to your fax of... (*10 June*).
Thank you for your letter of... (*17 March*).
Further to your telephone enquiry,... (*I enclose our catalogue and price list*).

Apologizing

I am sorry... (*about the delay*).
I apologize... (*for not replying sooner*).

Requesting

We would appreciate it if you would... (*send us further details*).
Could you please... (*reserve two single rooms*)?
Please... (*send confirmation of this booking*).
Would you kindly... (*check the tickets*)?

Agreeing to requests

I would be | pleased to... (*attend the meeting*).
              | delighted to... (*act as consultant*).

Giving good news

I am | pleased to inform you that... (*your application has been approved*).
      | delighted to tell you that... (*the order has been confirmed*).

Giving bad news

I am afraid... (*the trip has been delayed*).
Unfortunately... (*the hotel is fully booked*).

Explaining reasons

This is | the result of... (*an urgent meeting on Thursday*).
        | due to... (*an annual conference here this week*).

Enclosing documents

I enclose... (*a copy of my book*).
Please find enclosed... (*airline tickets for Ms R Lanson*).

Closing remarks

Please | contact us again if... (*we can help in any way*).
        | let me know if... (*you require any further information*).
        | pass on my best wishes to... (*Bob Wyatt*).
        | give our kind regards to... (*Señor Curzón*).

Referring to future contact

I look forward to... (*meeting you*).
I very much look forward to... (*meeting you again*).
Looking forward to... (*seeing you soon*).

Asking

I'd like | some information on... (*hotels*).
| to ask you about... (*flights to Prague*).
| to know... (*how long the journey takes*).

Could | you tell me... (*how many flights a day there are*)?
Can |

Do you know... (*if the flight from Moscow has arrived yet*)?
Do you happen to know... (*what time the airport bus will leave*)?

Checking	Confirming
You **did** say...(*Tuesday*), didn't you?	
That's... (*the 12th of this month*), is it?	➡ Yes, that's right.
So... (*the flight leaves at eight fifteen*)?	
Sorry, did you say... (*thirteen* or *thirty*)?	➡ I said thirteen.

Showing you understand

I see.
Right. I've got that.
OK. I understand now.

Correcting information

Sorry, I made a mistake. It's... (*40*), not... (*400*).
Sorry. That's not correct. It should be... (*10.30*).

Interviewing language

Introducing a topic

Could I start by asking you about... (*the area of production*)?
Perhaps I could ask you first about...
I wonder if you could tell me...
Could we talk about... (*production methods*) now?

Statement questions

I imagine... (*a lot of the sherry that's produced is exported*). Is that the case?
So... (*all sherry comes from this area*)?
So if ... (*70% is exported*), then... (*only 30% is drunk in Spain*)?

Asking for more information

You say... (*tastes are changing*). Could you explain in what way?
Earlier you referred to... (*the* solera *system*). Could you describe how... (*the* solera *system works*)?
You said... (*a new image was needed*). Could you expand on that?

Asking for clarification

By... (*DO wine*), do you mean... (*the wine produced in classified areas*)?
Could you explain what you mean by... (*DO wine*)?

Introductions

May I introduce you to... (*Dr Petersen*)? (F)
I'd like to introduce you to... (*Tomas Tauber*).
Can I introduce myself? My name is/I'm ... (*Ralph Keller*).
Can I introduce... (*a colleague of mine*)? This is... (*Pedro Romera*).
I don't know if you remember me. We met... (*in Prague last year*).
Hello. I don't think we've met before. (I)
I don't think you two know each other, do you? (I)
Excuse me. Would you by any chance be... (*Signor Tavazzi*)?
Hello, you must be... (*Leena*). (I)

How do you do. ➡	How do you do.
Pleased to meet you. ➡	Pleased to meet you, too.
Please call me... (*Anna*). ➡	Then you must call me... (*Bertrand*).

Greetings

Good/Nice to see you again. I haven't seen you for ages!

How are you? ➡	Very well, thanks. And you?
How's work? ➡	Not too bad, thanks. Very busy.
How are things going? ➡	Fine, thanks. What about you?
How's business? ➡	Not too good, I'm afraid.

Invitations

Inviting

I'd like to invite you... (*to dinner*).
Would you like to join us for... (*lunch*)?
Would you like to... (*go to the theatre*)?
What about... (*going out for a meal*)? (I)

Accepting

Thank you. That would be very nice.
Thank you. I'd enjoy that.
Thanks. I'd love to.
That's a good idea. (I)

Declining

I'd love to but... (*I'm afraid I've
made another arrangement*).
That's kind of you but...
(*unfortunately I won't be able to.
I'm leaving*).
Thanks but... (*I can't. I'm too busy*). (I)

17

Chairing a meeting/discussion

Opening
Right. Shall we start?
OK. Let's start. (I)

Stating objectives
The aim of this meeting is to...
In this meeting we must decide first... and second...
We need to decide...
(*The pilot programme*) has to achieve two aims...

Beginning the discussion
So, what are your views?
(*Eric*), would you like to start?
Could you begin, (*Rosa*)?

Asking for clarification
Sorry, (*Rosa*), I don't quite follow you.
Could you explain what you mean by... ?
Could you explain that again?
Would you mind repeating that?
Could you go over that again?

Checking agreement
So, are we all in agreement?
Do we all agree then?

Moving on
Can we get back to the main point?
Good. Then let's move on to the next topic...

Interrupting
Just a minute, could I just ask something?
Before you go on, could I say something?
Excuse me. Could I come in here?

Summarizing
So, to sum up...
We've agreed that...

Concluding
Well, I think that's everything.
Is there anything else you want to discuss?

Closing
Good, let's call it a day, then.

Narrating a story

Beginning
Did I ever tell you about...
(*my holiday in the mountains*)?
The worst experience I ever had was...
(*on a plane to New York*).
I'll never forget the time... (*I lost my car keys*).
I had a real shock the other day when...
(*I arrived home*).
This rather strange thing happened to
me in... (*a shop near the office*).
Something really unusual happened not long ago.

Adding details
The worst thing was...
What was really frightening was... (*the landing*).
The funniest part was... (*when the police arrived*).
And do you know what happened next?
And after that you'll never guess what happened.
What we didn't realize was...
(*it was the wrong address*).

Listening to a story

Reacting
Really?
How amusing!
That sounds really frightening!
That's really embarrassing!
How extraordinary!
How awful!

Asking for more details
When was that?
So what did you do?
Did you discover how... (*you lost them*)?
Why didn't you... (*go somewhere else*)?
How did you feel?
What happened in the end?

Commenting
Well, we all live and learn.
What an amazing coincidence!

Opinions

Asking for opinions
What are your views...
(*on the location*)?
What's your opinion...
(*of the hotel*)?
What do you think...
(*about the design*)?
How do you feel...
(*about John's proposal*)?
Do you think...
(*we need more information*)?

Giving opinions
I'm (*quite*) sure...
(*it's the best option*). (S)
I really do think...
(*we need more research*). (S)
From a (*financial*) point of view...
(*it should be very profitable*).
In my opinion... (*it's too expensive*).
I think... (*it's an excellent idea*).
I'm inclined to think...
(*it won't work*). (T)

Agreeing
Yes, I agree completely. (S)
Yes, definitely. (S)
I agree.
I'd go along with that.
Yes, you have a point there.

Disagreeing
In my opinion that's out of the question. (S)
I'm afraid I disagree completely. (S)
I'm afraid I can't agree with that idea.
Sorry, but I don't agree.
I'm afraid I don't really agree.
I'm afraid that's not how I see it.

Expressing reservations and doubts
I agree up to a point, but... (*we need more information*).
You could be right, but... (*it's very risky*).
Maybe, but... (*I think you should speak to him first*).

Requests and offers

Requesting

Could you possibly... (*call him*)?
Do you think you could... (*come too*)?
Would you... (*ring the company*)?
Could you... (*translate this*), please?
Can you... (*give me a hand*)?(I)

Would
Do | you mind... (*checking it*)? →

Offering

Would you like me to... (*book a room*)?
If you like, I can... (*find out*).
Shall I... (*change the flight*)?
Do you want me to... (*call her*)? (I)
Would you like... (*a lift*)?
Can I get you a drink? (I)
Do you need a hand? (I)

Agreeing

Yes, certainly.
Yes, that's no problem. →
Yes, of course.
Yes, I'll do that.

No, of course not. →
Not at all.

Refusing

I'm sorry but that's not possible...
(*It's too late*).
I'm afraid not... (*I have to go now*). →
I think that will be very difficult...
(*I'm very busy*).
Sorry, but... (*I'm too busy*). (I)

Accepting

Thanks. I'd appreciate that.
That's very kind of you.
Thanks, if you're sure it's no trouble. →
Yes, please. Thanks very much.

Declining

Thanks, but that won't be necessary.
That's very kind of you but... (*I can* →
manage).
Thanks, but please don't bother.

Saying goodbye

I must be going now... (*or I'll miss my plane*).
I really must be getting back to the office.
I think I should get back to my hotel now... (*as I'm leaving very early tomorrow*).
I must be off.

It's been very interesting I have enjoyed	meeting you. →	I've enjoyed meeting you, too.
I hope you have Have	a good	flight. trip. weekend.	→ →	Thanks... (*and the same to you*). Thanks... (*you too*). (I)
I hope to meet you again.		→	I hope so, too.

Thank you so much for all your hospitality.
Thanks very much for inviting me out to lunch. I've really enjoyed it.
Thank you for a really excellent meal.
Thank you very much for all your help. I really appreciate it.

I'm looking I look	forward to... (*meeting you again*).

Bye. See you I'll be in touch	on (*3 May*). soon.

Social responses

Invitations and offers

Would you like to come to our barbecue? ➡ I'd love to, but I'll be away then.
How about joining us tomorrow evening? ➡ That sounds like a good idea.

Do you fancy another drink? (I) ➡ Thank you. I'd like some more wine.
Do try one of these canapés. ➡ Thanks, but I couldn't eat anything else.
How do you like your coffee? ➡ Black, one sugar, please./White, please.
Would you like a lift? ➡ That's very kind of you, if it's no bother.

Responding politely

Oh, dear. I've just spilt some wine. ➡ Never mind.
I'm afraid Sara couldn't come. ➡ Oh, I'm sorry to hear that.
Antonio sends his regards. ➡ Thank you. Do give him mine.
I hope you have a good weekend. ➡ Thanks. The same to you.
I hope the next programme goes well. ➡ Thanks. I hope so too.

I'm afraid I didn't catch your name. ➡ It's Claire. Claire Hallan.
Do you mind if I open this window? ➡ Not at all.

Common expressions

Talking of... (*holidays, have you made any plans for next summer*)?
By the way,... (*we've managed to get tickets for the match on Sunday*).
As I was saying,... (*their daughter has just started her own business*).
That reminds me,... (*I must get in touch with him again*).
If you ask me,... (*I think he's making a big mistake*).
As you say,... (*the economic situation isn't getting any better*).

Talks and presentations

Introducing the topic
This morning I'm going to... (*talk about...*)/Today I'd like to... (*describe...*)
The aim of my presentation this morning is to... (*explain...*)
I've divided my presentation into... /My talk will be in...(*three parts*).
First, I'd like to... (*give you an overview of...*)
Second, I'll move on to.../Then I'll focus on...
After that we'll deal with.../Finally, we'll consider...

Referring to questions
Feel free to/Do interrupt me if there's anything you don't understand.
If you don't mind, we'll leave questions till the end.

Introducing each section
So, let's start with... (*the objectives...*)
Now let's move on to... (*the next part...*)
Let's turn our attention to... (*the question of...*)
This leads me to... (*my third point...*)
Finally,... (*let's consider...*)

Summarizing a section
That completes my... (*description of...*)/So, to summarize,... (*there are five key points...*)`

Referring
I mentioned earlier... (*the importance of...*)
I'll say more about this later./We'll come back to this point later.

Checking understanding
Is that clear?/Are there any questions?

Referring to visual information
This transparency/diagram shows...
If you look at this graph you can see.../What is interesting in this slide is...
I'd like to draw your attention to... (*this chart...*)

Referring to common knowledge
As you know.../As I'm sure you are aware...

Concluding
That concludes my talk./That brings me to the end of my presentation.
If you have any questions, I'd be pleased/I'll do my best to answer them.
Thank you for your attention.

Dealing with questions
That's a good point./I'm glad you asked that question.
Can I get back to you on that later? I'm afraid I don't have... (*the information at present*)./I'm afraid I'm not the right person to answer that.

Telephoning

Making contact
Hello. This is... (*Claire Hallan*).

Is that... (*Rosa*)?	➡	Yes, speaking.
Could I speak to... (*Mr Ames*)?	➡	Who's calling, please?

I'm | calling / phoning | about... (*the meeting*).

I'm sorry, the line is busy. Will you hold?

I'm afraid... (*Mr Dean*) isn't available today.

Leaving a message
Would you like to leave a message?

Shall I ask... (*him*) to ring you?

Could I leave a message?

Could you | ask... (*her*) to call... (*Bob Dunn*)? / tell... (*him*) that... (*James*) called?

Could you spell... (*your name*), please?

Making an appointment

When | would be convenient for you? / would suit you? / would be possible for you?

What time | could we meet? / are you free?

Would... (*Tuesday*) be convenient?	➡	Yes... (*Tuesday*) would be fine.
Could you manage... (*tomorrow*)?	➡	Yes... (*tomorrow*) suits me fine.
Shall we say... (*10 a.m.*)?	➡	Yes, I can make it then.
Can you make it... (*in the afternoon*)?	➡	No, I'm afraid I'm not available then.
Is... (*3 p.m.*) possible for you?	➡	No, I'm afraid I'm busy then.

Changing an appointment
I'm sorry, I have to cancel the appointment on... (*Monday*).

I'm afraid I can't manage our meeting... (*next week*).

I'm sorry, but... (*Piet*) isn't available... (*at that time*).

Could we arrange another time?

Welcoming a visitor

The visitor's journey
Did you have a good flight?
How was your journey?
I hope you had a good trip.
How long was the flight?
Did you have any problems finding us?

The visit
Is this your first visit to... (*Prague*)?
Have you been to... (*Brussels*) before?
What do you think of... (*the city*)?
Do you like... (*the food*)?
Are you here on business/holiday?
How long are you here for?

Accommodation
Where are you staying?
What's your hotel like?
I hope everything is OK at the hotel?

Weather
What was the weather like when you
left... (*Toronto*)?
What's the weather been like in...
(*England*)?
Isn't this weather wonderful/terrible?

Home town/country
Which part of... (*Canada*) are you from?
Where in... (*France*) do you live?
Which part of the city/country is that?
Where were you born?
Have you always lived in... (*London*)?

Work
What do you do?
Who do you work for?
Where are you based?
How long have you been with... (*the
company*)?

Travel and holidays
Do you often travel abroad?
Which countries do you visit?
Have you (ever) been to... (*Brazil*)?
Where did you spend your last holiday?

Interests
What do you do in your spare time?
How do you spend your weekends?
Are you interested in sport?

Current affairs
What's the latest news on... (*the hostage crisis*)?
What's the situation regarding... (*unemployment*)?
Is there any more news on... (*the elections*)?
Is... (*crime*) a serious problem?
Is the government tackling the problem of... (*terrorism*)?
Do you think... (*the political situation*) will change?

Dates and numbers

Dates

15 May		May 15	
15th May	*The fifteenth of May*	May 15th	*May the fifteenth*

- When we say the date, we use ordinal numbers. *June (the) twenty-third*; *December (the) eighth*.
- *May fifteenth*; *June twenty-third*, etc. is also possible, especially in American English.
- In the short form, the month is written before the day in American English. *7/3/97: 3 July 1997* (US); *7/3/97: 7 March 1997* (UK).

Fractions, decimals, and percentages

$^1/_2$ *a/one half*
$^2/_3$ *two thirds*
$^3/_4$ *three quarters*
$^1/_5$ *a/one fifth*

- With numbers less than one, we use *of* before a noun phrase. *A third of the money was paid in advance.*
- With numbers above one, we use a plural noun. *The office is one and a half miles from the station.*

2.7   *two point seven*
38.96   *thirty-eight point nine six*
9.04   *nine point oh/nought* four*
25.3%   *twenty-five point three per cent*

- After a decimal point we say each number separately.
- Americans* usually say *zero* rather than *oh*.

Describing your company or organization

I work for...	(*It*) was	founded established	in...

(*It*)	is (100)% owned by... belongs to...

(*It*)	produces... sells... provides... specializes in...	(*It*)	employs... has... employees	(*world-wide*).

(*Its*) annual turnover is...	(*It*) is located The headquarters are There are subsidiaries	in...

Present trends

People are	drinking	less	wine.
		a lot less	
	eating	more	convenience food.
		a lot more	

Fewer			smoking.
A lot fewer	people are		
More			buying microwaves.
A lot more			

Past trends

Wine consumption	increased	by	6%.
	rose		200 litres a month.
	declined		
	fell		

There was	an increase	of	5%.
	a rise		$10.
	a decline	in	the birth rate.
	a fall		market share.

- Verb + *by* (*decreased by $40*)
- Noun + *of* + amount (*a decrease of $40/500/60%*)
- Noun + *in* + topic (*a decrease in inflation/the cost of living/sales*)

Irregular verbs

Infinitive	Past	Participle	Infinitive	Past	Participle
be	was/were	been	catch	caught	caught
beat	beat	beaten	choose	chose	chosen
become	became	become	come	came	come
begin	began	begun	cost	cost	cost
bend	bent	bent	cut	cut	cut
bite	bit	bitten	deal	dealt	dealt
blow	blew	blown	do	did	done
break	broke	broken	draw	drew	drawn
bring	brought	brought	drink	drank	drunk
build	built	built	drive	drove	driven
buy	bought	bought	eat	ate	eaten

fall	fell	fallen	say	said	said
feed	fed	fed	see	saw	seen
feel	felt	felt	sell	sold	sold
fight	fought	fought	send	sent	sent
find	found	found	set	set	set
fly	flew	flown	sew	sewed	sewn
forbid	forbade	forbidden	shake	shook	shaken
forget	forgot	forgotten	shine	shone	shone
forgive	forgave	forgiven	shoot	shot	shot
freeze	froze	frozen	show	showed	shown
get	got	got	shrink	shrank	shrunk
give	gave	given	shut	shut	shut
go	went	gone	sing	sang	sung
grow	grew	grown	sink	sank	sunk
hang	hung	hung	sit	sat	sat
have	had	had	sleep	slept	slept
hear	heard	heard	slide	slid	slid
hide	hid	hidden	speak	spoke	spoken
hit	hit	hit	spend	spent	spent
hold	held	held	split	split	split
hurt	hurt	hurt	spread	spread	spread
keep	kept	kept	stand	stood	stood
know	knew	known	steal	stole	stolen
lay	laid	laid	stick	stuck	stuck
lead	led	led	strike	struck	struck
leave	left	left	swear	swore	sworn
lend	lent	lent	sweep	swept	swept
lie	lay	lain	swim	swam	swum
light	lit	lit	take	took	taken
lose	lost	lost	teach	taught	taught
make	made	made	tear	tore	torn
mean	meant	meant	tell	told	told
meet	met	met	think	thought	thought
pay	paid	paid	throw	threw	thrown
put	put	put	understand	understood	understood
read	read	read	wake	woke	woken
ride	rode	ridden	wear	wore	worn
ring	rang	rung	win	won	won
rise	rose	risen	write	wrote	written
run	ran	run			

Cause/reason
because of + noun
because + clause

- We use *because of* before a noun. *The Socialists were expected to lose votes **because of** a corruption scandal.*
- We use *because* before a clause. *The Socialists were expected to lose votes **because** they had failed to deal with the problems.*

Contrast
although + clause   *despite/in spite of* + noun or *-ing* form of verb (gerund)
however + sentence   *despite/in spite of the fact that* + clause

- We use *although, in spite of, despite,* and *in spite of the fact that* to link two clauses. ***Although** voting is compulsory, the electorate showed little interest in the election campaign. The government is expected to remain in power, **although** it is unpopular.*
- We cannot use *however* to link two clauses. *Voting is compulsory. **However**, the electorate showed little interest in the election campaign.*
- We use *despite* and *in spite of* in the same way, and with the same meaning. ***Despite/In spite of** being unpopular, the governing centre-left coalition is expected to remain in power.*
- We can use *in spite of the fact that* in the same way as *although. The governing centre-left coalition is expected to remain in power, **in spite of the fact that/although** it is unpopular.*

Phonetic symbols

Vowels

iː	as in	see /siː/	ʊ	as in	put /pʊt/	aɪ	as in	five /faɪv/
ɪ	as in	sit /sɪt/	uː	as in	too /tuː/	aʊ	as in	now /naʊ/
e	as in	ten /ten/	ʌ	as in	cup /kʌp/	ɔɪ	as in	join /dʒɔɪn/
æ	as in	hat /hæt/	ɜː	as in	fur /fɜː(r)/	ɪə	as in	near /nɪə(r)/
ɑː	as in	arm /ɑːm/	ə	as in	ago /əˈɡəʊ/	eə	as in	hair /heə(r)/
ɒ	as in	got /ɡɒt/	eɪ	as in	page /peɪdʒ/	ʊə	as in	pure /pjʊə(r)/
ɔː	as in	saw /sɔː/	əʊ	as in	home /həʊm/			

Consonants

p	as in	pen /pen/	f	as in	fall /fɔːl/	h	as in	how /haʊ/
b	as in	bad /bæd/	v	as in	voice /vɔɪs/	m	as in	man /mæn/
t	as in	tea /tiː/	θ	as in	thin /θɪn/	n	as in	no /nəʊ/
d	as in	did /dɪd/	ð	as in	then /ðen/	ŋ	as in	sing /sɪŋ/
k	as in	cat /kæt/	s	as in	so /səʊ/	l	as in	leg /leɡ/
ɡ	as in	got /ɡɒt/	z	as in	zoo /zuː/	r	as in	red /red/
tʃ	as in	chin /tʃɪn/	ʃ	as in	she /ʃiː/	j	as in	yes /jes/
dʒ	as in	June /dʒuːn/	ʒ	as in	vision /ˈvɪʒn/	w	as in	wet /wet/

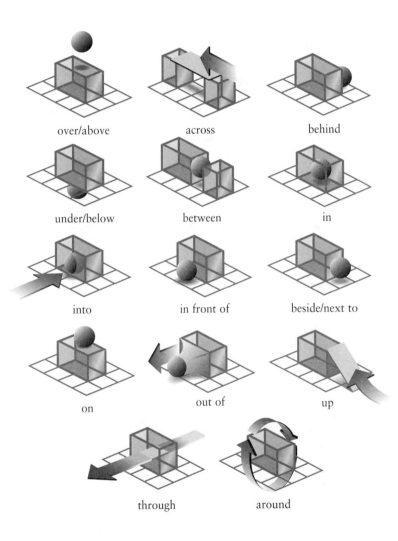

over/above   across   behind

under/below   between   in

into   in front of   beside/next to

on   out of   up

through   around

Past Simple

Past Continuous

Past Perfect

used to

Present Perfect Simple

Present Perfect Simple with *ever*

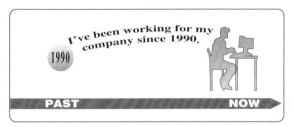

Present Perfect Continuous

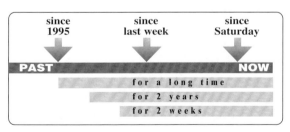

for/since

Oxford University Press
Great Clarendon Street, Oxford OX2 6DP

Oxford New York
Athens Auckland Bangkok Bogota Bombay
Buenos Aires Calcutta Cape Town Dar es Salaam
Delhi Florence Hong Kong Istanbul Karachi
Kuala Lumpur Madras Madrid Melbourne
Mexico City Nairobi Paris Singapore
Taipei Tokyo Toronto Warsaw

and associated companies in
Berlin Ibadan

OXFORD and OXFORD ENGLISH
are trade marks of Oxford University Press

ISBN 0 19 435669 8

© Oxford University Press 1997

First published 1997
Second impression 1997

No unauthorized photocopying

Printed in Hong Kong

Illustrations by Oliver Hutton